BIOGRAPHIES

ABRAHAM LINCOLN

by Laura K. Murray

PEBBLE
a capstone imprint

Pebble Explore is published by Pebble, an imprint of Capstone.
1710 Roe Crest Drive
North Mankato, Minnesota 56003
www.capstonepub.com

Library of Congress Cataloging-in-Publication data is available on the Library of Congress website.
ISBN: 978-1-9771-1357-3 (library binding)
ISBN: 978-1-9771-1801-1 (paperback)
ISBN: 978-1-9771-1365-8 (eBook PDF)

Summary: Explores the life, challenges, and accomplishments of Abraham Lincoln, the 16th president of the United States.

Image Credits
iStockphoto: benoitb, 13, ilbusca, 7; Library of Congress: 5, 10, 18, 21, 27, 29; Newscom: Frances M. Roberts, 24, Glasshouse Images, 14, Picture History/ Anthony Berger, 15, World History Archive, 8; Shutterstock: Alex Landa (geometric background), cover, back cover, 2, 29, Everett Historical, cover, 1, 11, 12, 16, 17, Robynrg, 25 (bottom), Spiroview Inc, 25 (top), VIIIPhotography, 26; The Metropolitan Museum of Art: Gilman Collection, Purchase, The Horace W. Goldsmith Foundation Gift, through Joyce and Robert Menschel, 2005, 23

Editorial Credits
Christopher Harbo, editor; Elyse White, designer; Jo Miller, media researcher; Katy LaVigne, production specialist

All internet sites appearing in back matter were available and accurate when this book was sent to press.

Printed in the United States 6520

Table of Contents

Words in **bold** are in the glossary.

Who Was Abraham Lincoln?

Abraham Lincoln was the 16th **president** of the United States. He led the country through hard times. Abraham was president during the U.S. Civil War (1861–1865). This war almost split the United States in two.

Abraham worked hard all of his life. He helped end **slavery** in the United States. Many people believe he was the best president the country ever had.

Growing Up Abraham

Abraham Lincoln was born more than 200 years ago on February 12, 1809. He had an older sister named Sarah. His family lived in a one-room cabin on a farm in Kentucky. When Abraham was 2, his family moved to Knob Creek Farm a few miles away.

Abraham's family was very poor. They moved to Indiana when he was 7. Abraham's mother died two years later. His father married again. Abraham's stepmother was very kind.

Abraham's first home

Abraham worked a lot while growing up. He chopped wood and took care of the farm animals. He did not get to go to school much. But he liked to learn and read. He always had a book with him.

Abraham worked on a river boat as a teenager. Then he built his own boat. He took crops down the Mississippi River. He gave his family the money he made.

Family and Hobbies

Abraham moved to Illinois at age 21. He worked in a store and as a soldier. Then Abraham taught himself to be a **lawyer**. He helped people with law problems. He was honest and kind. People called him "Honest Abe."

Abraham as a lawyer

Mary Todd Lincoln

Abraham married Mary Todd in 1842. They had four sons. Their names were Robert, Edward, Willie, and Tad. Edward died very young. And in 1862, Willie died at age 11. This was very hard for the Lincoln family.

Abraham had many hobbies. He liked to tell jokes and funny stories. He liked reading books and writing poems. Sometimes he played chess. He and his family had cats, dogs, rabbits, and goats.

Abraham read to his family.

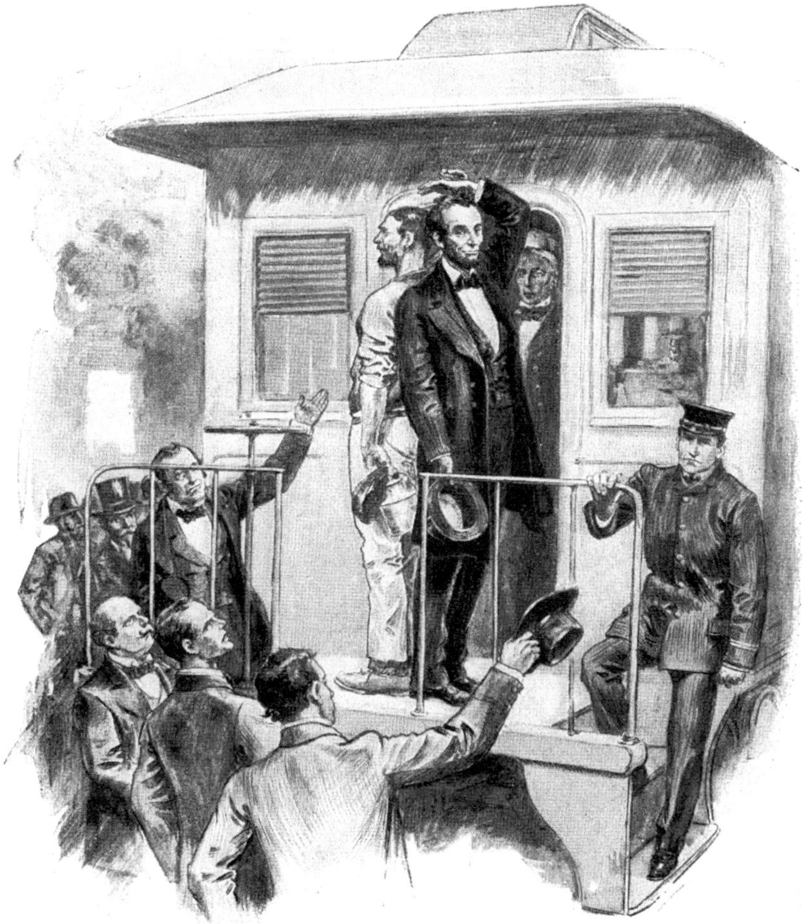

Abraham was very tall. He stood 6 feet, 4 inches (193 centimeters) tall. He often wore a tall black hat, called a stovepipe hat. It made him look even taller.

Honest Abe

In 1834, Abraham started working in state **government**. Twelve years later, he became a U.S. **representative**. In 1860, Abraham ran for president at age 51. He won, but many people were unhappy about this.

Abraham gave a speech in 1858.

Abraham in the White House

Abraham believed that **enslaving** people was wrong. He did not want slavery to spread to any more states.

Leaders of some southern states were angry that Abraham wouldn't let slavery spread to more states. They wanted to make their own country so that they could keep slavery.

Abraham wanted to keep the country together. But 11 southern states broke away. They formed the Confederate States of America. Soon the Civil War began. Abraham led the Union against the Confederate states.

Abraham met with Union soldiers in 1862.

Abraham worked on the Emancipation Proclamation.

On January 1, 1863, Abraham issued the Emancipation Proclamation. It said enslaved people in Confederate states were now free. Slaveholders did not listen. But when Union armies won battles in the South, they freed enslaved people along the way.

Abraham's Gettysburg Address

Abraham worked to keep the Union strong. He gave many speeches. One of his most famous speeches was the Gettysburg Address. He gave it on November 19, 1863, after the Union won an important battle at Gettysburg, Pennsylvania. His words would be remembered forever.

Abraham became president again in 1864. The states were still fighting. Abraham wanted to pass an **amendment** to the **U.S. Constitution**. This change would make slavery against the law in the United States.

The War Ends

On April 9, 1865, the long war ended. More than 600,000 people had died, but the Union won. It meant the United States would be one country again. Abraham made plans to help make it stronger.

Five days later, Abraham and Mary went to a play in Washington, D.C. As they sat in Ford's Theatre, a man named John Wilkes Booth shot Abraham. Booth was angry the Union won the war. Abraham died the next morning at age 56.

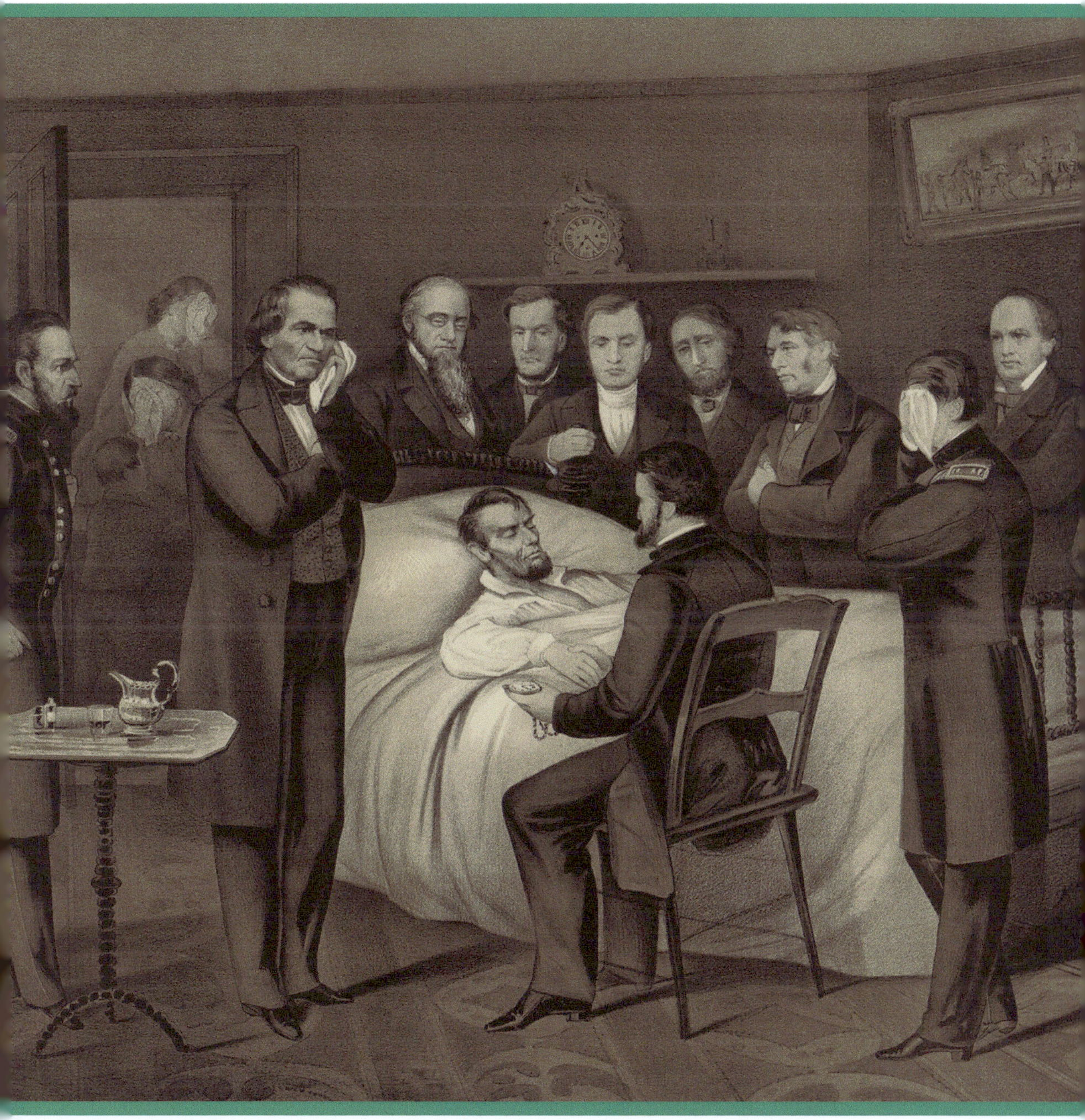

A train took Abraham's body from Washington, D.C., to Springfield, Illinois. It stopped in many cities along the way. People came to say goodbye. In early May, Abraham was buried.

Even though Abraham had died, the work to end slavery kept going. In December 1865, the 13th Amendment ended slavery in the United States. Sadly, Abraham did not get to see it.

Abraham's
funeral train

Remembering Lincoln

Today people remember Abraham's life. Some states remember his birthday on February 12. People also think of him on June 19 each year. On this holiday, called Juneteenth, people remember the end of slavery.

People remember Abraham when they go places and use money. Many schools and streets are named after him. The capital of Nebraska is named Lincoln. Abraham's face is also on the penny and the $5 bill.

People go many places to learn more about Abraham. They can learn about his time as president at a library and museum in Springfield, Illinois. They can also see the Lincoln **Memorial** in Washington, D.C. It has a huge statue of Abraham.

Lincoln Memorial

People remember Abraham Lincoln as a hero. He was born poor. He worked hard to help his family make a living. He led the United States through war. Abraham believed in freedom and helped end slavery in the United States.

Important Dates

February 12, 1809	Abraham Lincoln is born in Kentucky.
November 4, 1842	Abraham marries Mary Todd.
August 3, 1846	Abraham becomes a U.S. representative.
November 6, 1860	Abraham is elected as the 16th president of the United States.
April 12, 1861	The Civil War begins. Lincoln leads the Union against the Confederate States of America.
January 1, 1863	Abraham issues the Emancipation Proclamation, freeing enslaved people in many Confederate states.
November 19, 1863	Abraham gives the Gettysburg Address in Gettysburg, Pennsylvania.
November 8, 1864	Abraham is elected U.S. president for a second time.
April 9, 1865	The Civil War ends. The Union wins.
April 14, 1865	Abraham is shot by John Wilkes Booth in Ford's Theatre in Washington, D.C. He dies the next day at the age of 56.
December 1865	The 13th Amendment ends slavery in the United States.

Fast Facts

Name:
Abraham Lincoln

Role:
16th president of the United States

Life dates:
February 12, 1809 to April 15, 1865

Key accomplishments:
Abraham Lincoln was the 16th president of the United States. He led the country through the Civil War. In 1863, his Emancipation Proclamation freed enslaved people in many southern states. Abraham also helped get the 13th Amendment to the U.S. Constitution passed. It ended slavery in the United States forever.

Glossary

amendment (uh-MEND-muhnt)—a change made to a law or a legal document

enslave (en-SLAYV)—to make someone lose their freedom

government (GUHV-urn-muhnt)—the group of people who make laws and decisions for a country or state

lawyer (LOI-ur)—a person who is trained to advise people about the law

memorial (muh-MOR-ee-uhl)—something that is built or done to help people remember a person or event

president (PREZ-uh-duhnt)—the highest elected job in a class, business, or country

representative (rep-ri-ZEN-tuh-tiv)—a person elected to serve the government; U.S. representatives serve in the House of Representatives

slavery (SLAY-vur-ee)—the practice of owning other people; slaves are forced to work without pay

U.S. Constitution (YOO ESS kahn-stuh-TOO-shuhn)—the plan for how the U.S. government works

Read More

Edison, Erin. *The Lincoln Memorial*. North Mankato, MN: Capstone, 2019.

Keating, Frank, and Mike Wimmer. *Abraham*. New York: Simon & Schuster Books for Young Readers, 2017.

Kirkman, Marissa. *The Life and Times of Abraham Lincoln and the U.S. Civil War*. North Mankato, MN: Capstone, 2017.

Internet Sites

Abraham Lincoln Presidential Library and Museum
http://lincolnlibraryandmuseum.com/index.htm

Abraham Lincoln: The White House
https://www.whitehouse.gov/about-the-white-house/presidents/abraham-lincoln/

Biography of Abraham Lincoln
https://www.ducksters.com/biography/uspresidents/abrahamlincoln.php

Index